EXECUTIVE STYLE

BY JUDITH PRICE

DESIGNED BY BOB CIANO

THE LINDEN PRESS/SIMON & SCHUSTER
NEW YORK 1980

Copyright © 1980 by Judith Price
Published by The Linden Press/Simon & Schuster
A Simon & Schuster Division of Gulf & Western Corporation
Simon & Schuster Building
1230 Avenue of the Americas
New York, New York 10020
THE LINDEN PRESS/SIMON & SCHUSTER and colophon are trademarks of
Simon & Schuster
Designed by Bob Ciano

Manufactured in the United States of America
Color Separations by Offset Separations, Inc.
Printed and Bound by Kingsport Press

1 3 5 7 9 10 8 6 4 2

Library of Congress Cataloging in Publication Data

Price, Judith, date.
Executive style.

1. Office decoration.   2. Executives.   I.   Title.
NK2195.04P74   747'.852   80-21738

ISBN 0-671-25354-9

ACKNOWLEDGMENTS

I want to thank all the executives who graciously allowed us to feature their offices in this book. And to convey my thanks to all the architects, designers, manufacturers, wholesalers and retailers who patiently answered my questions and offered advice and direction.

My particular thanks to the photographers whose pictures appear on the following pages and to the man who led us to them, Melvin L. Scott. To Henry Groskinsky (pages 12–26, 27 bottom, 54–71, 94–101, 108–111, 114, 115, 134–137, 140–145, 152, 153, 168–175, 182–187, 192, 193); Harry Benson (pages 11, 30, 31, 34, 36–39, 45–47, 50, 51, 75, 79, 88, 89, 90, 91, 117, 122–127, 130, 131, 133, 160–165, 167, 194–213 and end papers, front and back); Jerry Sarapochiello (pages 35, 40, 41, 43, 44, 72, 73, 74, 80, 81, 93, 116, 118–121); Michael Pateman (pages 32, 33, 48, 49, 53, 76–78, 84–87 and jacket photo); Larry Dale Gordon (pages 112, 113, 146–149); Jim Leviton (pages 28, 29, 106, 107); Arnold Zann (pages 27 top, 104, 105, 178–181, 188–191); Tom Tracy (pages 138, 139); Jim Olive (pages 176, 177); Carl Fischer (pages 82, 83, 128, 129); Jaime Ardiles-Arce (pages 156–159); Richard Payne (pages 102, 103) and Jeffrey Folinus (pages 150, 151, 154, 155).

To Mallory Samson, my research assistant, who supervised many a photography session and kept me constantly organized.

To Mary Dunphy and Grace Karl for their seemingly endless supply of staunch support and tireless assistance, and to Madlyn Deming for being on call for all the last-minute details.

A special thanks to Joni Evans, my editor, who provided the necessary faith and cheered me on the finish.

And, of course, to Bob Ciano, whose good taste and superb design have helped to make this book what it is.

—Judith Price

CONTENTS

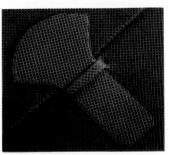

Any successful company has known about style for years. Style makes whatever you sell distinctive—and better than somebody else's product. Style is quality, innovation; but it's also design, advertising, packaging. It's what makes your company and its product stand out in a crowd. ☐ The chairman or president, designer or director behind a product can stand out, too. Executive style need not be blatant—unless you're a Rothschild and can afford to keep a functioning spittoon in your office, or, like power pundit Michael Korda, you make the rules and therefore can break them. (Mr. Korda's decor features a collection of helmets and a gallery of equestrian memorabilia.) But neither is it simply good taste or design. "An ax handle doesn't have style," said Mies van der Rohe. "It has beauty and appropriateness of form and a this-is-how-it-should-be-ness, but it has no style because style reflects idiosyncrasies." Style is certainly not just money: A thousand-dollar attaché case with a designer's initials on it doesn't have much style at all. ☐ Style isn't something you're born with or something you acquire when you reach a certain age. It isn't something you earn if you live in a particular city or at a specific address. Style comes only from recognizing your own best traits and exhibiting them with taste and flair in everything you do. Style is what makes whoever you meet know you are unique. ☐ Executive style shows up in everything you as a successful executive do—the way you entertain, the way you travel, the team you hire. But one part of your work life conveys executive style better than anything else: your office. Not long ago, most executives thought that caring about how an office looked was frivolous, money-wasting, unbusinesslike. But most executives didn't care what color shirt they wore, either, so long as it was white, or about the length of their hair, so long as it was the same as everybody else's. ☐ Now in even the most conservative professions, that corporate uniform has come to mark its wearer for what he is: bland, boring, and behind the times. A good executive, says management expert Peter Drucker, exists to make sensible exceptions to general rules. That makes executives with style neither followers nor outsiders, but leaders—confident and decisive. People succeeding in business today know how to distinguish themselves, and they know that one place to do that with style is in the room where they work. Not that they're running to decorators for the latest in Ultrasuede couches. Indeed, executive style may ignore trends altogether: David Rockefeller's office has stayed the same since 1961.

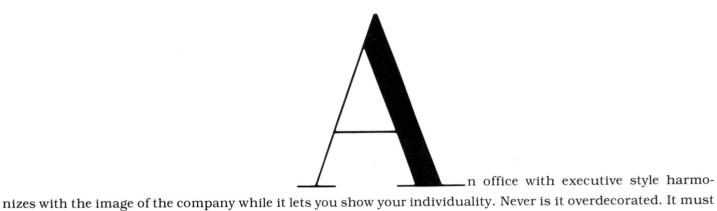

An office with executive style harmonizes with the image of the company while it lets you show your individuality. Never is it overdecorated. It must set you off but not dominate you, reflect you but not overpower you. An office should be a *frame* for your personality; a giant desk or a massive chair, for example, makes so strong a statement it pushes you out of the picture. A raft of family photographs may transmit too much intimacy; a wall full of diplomas and awards signals insecurity to more people than it impresses. ☐ Your office should be a happy and comfortable place. It should force you to be more creative, more energetic. It should tell everyone who walks in—your boss, your colleagues, your staff, your clients—that you care about your work. Above all, your office should be a haven. Management experts estimate that executives spend twice as many of their waking hours in their offices as they do in their homes. Your spouse's tastes aren't reflected here, or your kids' fingermarks, or your dog's hair. Even if your furniture is regulation-issue, you can make your office your own and make your mark with style. Style can be a daisy in a vase, a cushion on a couch, sandwiches served on a black lacquer tray instead of a cardboard carton. If you're lucky enough to have money and freedom, style can be anything you want it to be. ☐ The offices and objects pictured in this book prove that style isn't a matter of office size or size of budget, of period of furniture or brand of carpeting. Each office in this book showcases an individual—from Estée Lauder with her drawing-room romanticism to the captain's-bridge sleekness of Oppenheimer & Company's chairman, Jack Nash. The rooms were chosen from nearly a thousand offices suggested by leading architectural and design firms across the country, and were selected in consultation with leaders of the architectural and design community. Unlike catalogues of office furniture, the presentation here ranges across periods, manufacturers, and styles (although, like a catalogue, it does include a directory, with prices as current as inflation permits). ☐ Yet *Executive Style* is not a book about interior decorating. Instead, it's a book about exterior reflection. Not every desk or chair or table, attaché case or fountain pen would be right for who you are—that's just the point of executive style. But every object has the clean lines and good design that project strength, directness, and competence, the basis on which you as an executive can build your own individual style.

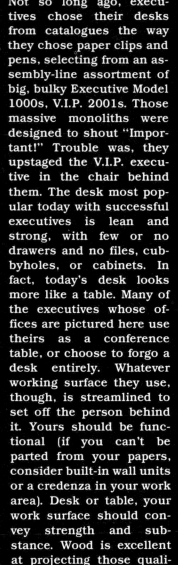

Not so long ago, executives chose their desks from catalogues the way they chose paper clips and pens, selecting from an assembly-line assortment of big, bulky Executive Model 1000s, V.I.P. 2001s. Those massive monoliths were designed to shout "Important!" Trouble was, they upstaged the V.I.P. executive in the chair behind them. The desk most popular today with successful executives is lean and strong, with few or no drawers and no files, cubbyholes, or cabinets. In fact, today's desk looks more like a table. Many of the executives whose offices are pictured here use theirs as a conference table, or choose to forgo a desk entirely. Whatever working surface they use, though, is streamlined to set off the person behind it. Yours should be functional (if you can't be parted from your papers, consider built-in wall units or a credenza in your work area). Desk or table, your work surface should convey strength and substance. Wood is excellent at projecting those qualities. Other materials—

stone, steel, leather, even Formica and glass—can establish distinction without dandyism.

Does that mean you have to spend a fortune for a desk? Not really, though here, as everywhere, you get what you pay for. Look for clean lines and honest design and materials. What doesn't convey solidity and propriety is a material that tries to be something it's not—Naugahyde that's masquerading as leather, plastic that's trying (and failing) to be wood. If you're after a traditional desk, though, don't turn up your nose at reproductions. Distressed wood, which badly counterfeits the look of an antique, is the sort of thing you want to avoid. But a careful reproduction, constructed of good materials, is to be considered if you can't afford an original design of the past.

Bob Fomon, Chief Executive Officer of E. F. Hutton & Company, the country's second-largest brokerage house, can't be pinned down to one desk. Three areas create three different office environments, and three table shapes serve different needs. An antique Regency desk anchors the room; in contrast, a contemporary rosewood and lacquer table for the formal conference area; and finally, a honed granite and Kortan steel coffee table for the informal meeting area. The unexpected use of the Pirelli rubber tile floor with the antique Heriz is both practical—Mr. Fomon loves to pace—and elegant.

An office doesn't have to be large to be grand. It doesn't even have to have a window. But what furniture there is in the office, above, of Erwin Isman, President of Perry Ellis Sportswear, is choice—chairs designed by Eames and Mies van der Rohe, and a hand-lacquered English sycamore desk that achieves the proportions of sculpture. The offices had formerly been a bank, and the marble column behind Mr. Isman's desk was deservedly retained to enhance this environment. The tinted glass walls give light and privacy in one stroke, and also enlarge the room. At right, Mr. Isman's secretary's office prepares the visitor for the understated elegance that lies behind his office door.

In 1917, Mrs. Morton Plant traded her townhouse on Fifth Avenue and Fifty-second Street in Manhattan to Cartier for a string of pearls valued at one million dollars. The mansion now houses the office of Cartier president Ralph Destino, in a room that preserves without embalming its original grandeur. Mr. Destino's desk and desk chairs demonstrate that rules about gender aren't sacred when it comes to choosing office furniture. The elegant Louis Quinze-styled desk and desk chairs are undeniably masculine, belying the notion that French furniture goes best in the boudoir. Nor must one follow outdated rules against mixing periods—the contemporary upholstered club chair by the window blends in perfectly. The Cartier plaque was once on the façade of the building. (Cartier, incidentally, got the better of that trade with Mrs. Plant. With the advent of cultured pearls, prices plummeted, and at her death in 1956, Mrs. Plant's pearls fetched some $150,000 at auction.)

17

The desk pictured here is the most massive in this book, but Walter Hoving, chairman of Tiffany & Co., wouldn't be dwarfed by a redwood. The eighteenth-century mahogany partners' desk is flanked by three Chippendale armchairs; the bowls on the desk are Lowestoft, and the box and engagement book cover are vermeil. The wood paneling and overhead light lend an aura of strength and permanence.

If ever an office expressed its occupant's taste, it's that of cosmetics czarina Estée Lauder, and only a secure personality (that is, someone who owns the show) can afford quite this much individuality. But the result here is glorious—a lush, opulent office that outshines the most luxurious drawing rooms. The Louis XVI desk is the centerpiece of a salon that mixes European periods, patterns, furniture, and accessories. The walls, covered with hand-painted Oriental rice paper, add to the effect.

The office of Ira Howard Levy, Senior Vice President of Corporate Marketing-Design of Estée Lauder, is centuries removed in feeling from his boss's, but no less arresting. Mr. Levy uses small space to optimum advantage, choosing each detail with exacting discernment. The cantilevered desk attests to the maxim that less is more. From the front, one would not imagine this trim desk could support the luxury of a drawer (pictured above). The desk chair is upholstered in seal-colored Hermes leather. All this perfection has not made Mr. Levy lose his touch of humor. The screwdriver sculpture is a touch of whimsy that some, if not all, offices could tolerate.

Three very different offices with three very different desks—yet all of them work in their environment, functionally and as elements of design. At left is the office of United Match Corporation's chairman and president, H. Ridgely Bullock. Here the mahogany, eighteenth-century-styled English desk echoes its traditional surroundings. At top right is the Chicago office of Banco di Roma's chairman, John T. Rettaliata. The desk here is of African rosewood trimmed in polished stainless steel, repeating the straight and geometric lines of the office. (Square and round desks are unusual in that they have no designated "power seat"; if you like the idea of an office democracy, this device is ideal.) Below right, the striking leather and chrome desk of advertising agency Nadler & Larimer's chairman, Arch Nadler, is the focal point of his strong, modern office.

Not every office has to have a desk. Edward E. Elson, the president of Elson's and Atlanta News Agency, designed this stainless-steel-paneled room without one. In its stead, he uses the white marble cube and the octagonal art deco telephone table. Collecting is a hobby of Mr. Elson's, and the office enhances some of his most prized pieces: in the glass-enclosed cabinets are vases by Primavera, brass and steel figures by K. Hagenauer, bookends by Chase, a Lalique decanter, and a Muller Frères flask. The marble cube sits on an eighteenth-century Chinese rug and is surrounded by six Le Corbusier club chairs and a Le Corbusier pony-skin lounge chair. True to his individualistic spirit, Mr. Elson has defied tradition and made his office a personal living room.

Strong and masculine may
not be words one associates
with Louis Quinze and Ro-
coco, but both fit this superb antique tulip wood
writing table from the
French firm of Didier
Aaron. Ormolu—the gold
leaf fused onto brass that
decorates the desk here—
was originated during the
eighteenth century to pro-
tect vulnerable corners and
hold veneer in place. The
table is from the Russian
Imperial Collection.

If the idea of a square desk intrigues you, consider this table by Brickel, with black enameled steel pedestal base and three-quarter-inch marble top. The table was designed in 1964 by Ward Bennett, whose work is noted for its purity of form. In its design, the base replicates a standard I-beam used in building construction but here the lines are softened to lend the table a subtle, timeless grace. The price is approximately $1500.

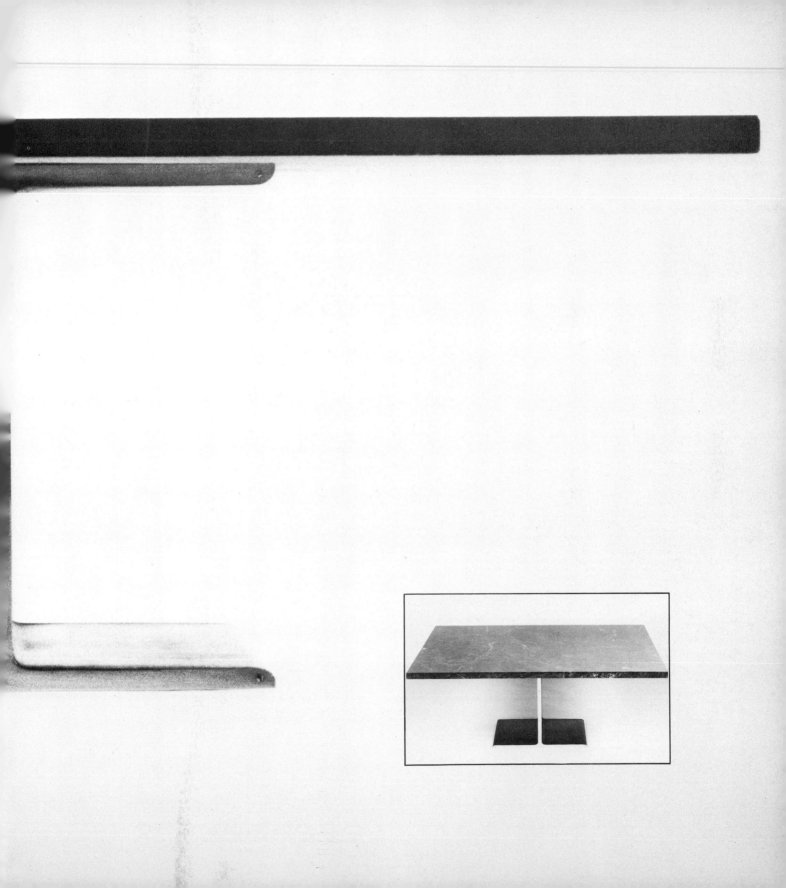

From Stair & Company, above, a beautifully grained and shaded mahogany English Chippendale double-sided writing table, c. 1760. The fret brackets are brass. Approximately $26,000. Compare it with the modern desk with granite top and leather base, by Dunbar, at right, which conveys an equivalent degree of style and solidity. The Dunbar desk, designed by de Polo/Dunbar, is also available with pedestals or with return; its top may be of marble or leather instead of granite, or the desk may be ordered entirely in oak or leather.

At the Hôtel du Collection-
neur of the Arts Décoratifs
exhibition held in Paris in
1925, when Europe still
was recovering from World
War I, the critics disap-
proved of the inappro-
priately luxurious creations
of Jacques Emile Ruhl-
mann, who favored rare
woods and ivory. Ruhlmann
explained that he cared to
design only for the very
rich. The tapering reeded
leg merging into the body is
his invention; the art deco
desk shown here is of rosewood veneer with ivory handles and is available from
Didier Aaron for nearly
$50,000.

CHAIRS

Unless you spend most of your time at the golf club, the first thing to look for in a desk chair is comfort. Trying to work well in an uncomfortable chair is like wearing tight shoes on a grand tour of Europe. But there's no reason nowadays not to have both comfort and style.

The perfect desk chair is one that doesn't disappear behind your desk but doesn't dominate the desk —or you—either. Those very high-backed executive chairs that used to be popular tend to dwarf a person and make him or her look silly, like a judge in the wrong courtroom. For a well-put-together look, the chairs in front of the desk should be of the same design as the ones behind it —not necessarily identical, but perhaps the same chair without arms, or in a slightly scaled-down version. Chairs or sofas elsewhere in the room need only not clash with those at the desk; variation and contrast give an office interest and style. As for color, generally go easy— bright colors and busy patterns tend to be distracting. Neutral, or at least muted, colors in fabrics of interesting texture make most executives happiest. An antique adds beauty, a sense of permanence, and a touch of your personality.

But antiques and upholstery bring us to another subject—upkeep. Few offices are blessed with a decent cleaning service. If you're one of the many executives who must make do with a quick emptying of the ashtrays and swipe of the dustcloth, think hard before you upholster in white velvet or purchase an antique that requires loving hand-polishing to look its best. Fortunately, the variety in easy-to-care-for fabrics and finishes now is as vast as the selection of chairs and sofas that can make your office a place where both you and your visitors want to spend time.

If one had to guess who concocted this flamboyantly sensual art deco fantasy, first choice would likely be fashion designer and entrepreneur Diane Von Furstenberg. She asked her designer for a mixture of transatlantic ocean liner and Esther Williams movie, and she got it. Perhaps the major element is the gray velvet art deco chairs—a blend of drop-dead elegance and sheer theater. But only a bigger-than-life person could get away with an office like this one—and with the visual laboratory above

the art nouveau desk. Art deco, with its ornate Persian influences, its often overwhelming abundance of zigzags and Lucite, may serve best in accent pieces —a lamp, a pillow, an ashtray.

The office of Xerox president David T. Kearns is a room with more than one advantage. Its neutral colors and clean lines transmit a feeling of comfort and restraint; the pastoral painting is pleasing but not overpowering. The Stendig sofa and lounge chairs in the meeting area are more customarily found in reception rooms—chairs that invite one to lean back and relax. For Mr. Kearns, they're an informal alternative to the nearby desk–conference table work area.

The chairs surrounding Mr. Kearns's desk are by Helikon, their upholstery by Scalamandré. The window treatment is minimal, putting as little as possible between Mr. Kearns and the view.

The couch and chairs in the office of John Marion, president of Sotheby Parke Bernet, are central in creating the relaxed, homelike environment here—important when many of the visitors are tensely thinking about parting with valuable possessions or even their family homes to this premier auction house. The mahogany armchairs are Regency antiques. The art on Mr. Marion's walls changes with the company's inventory. Shown here, reading clockwise from left: Pierre Bonnard, *Woman in a Bathtub*, circa 1917; Pierre-Auguste Renoir, *The Loge*, 1897; Renoir, *Bather Drying Her Feet*, circa 1907.

Ahmet Ertegun is chairman of Atlantic Recording
Corporation, and his Knoll chairs and side couches
have held the derrieres of superstars like Mick Jagger
and Led Zeppelin. The office, planned to convey the
feeling of a sitting room because Mr. Ertegun entertains
frequently here, also projects, with its classic Parsons
desk and sleek wall units, an atmosphere of cozy
efficiency. The bowl of orchids on the table adds, as
flowers always do, a further touch of warmth.

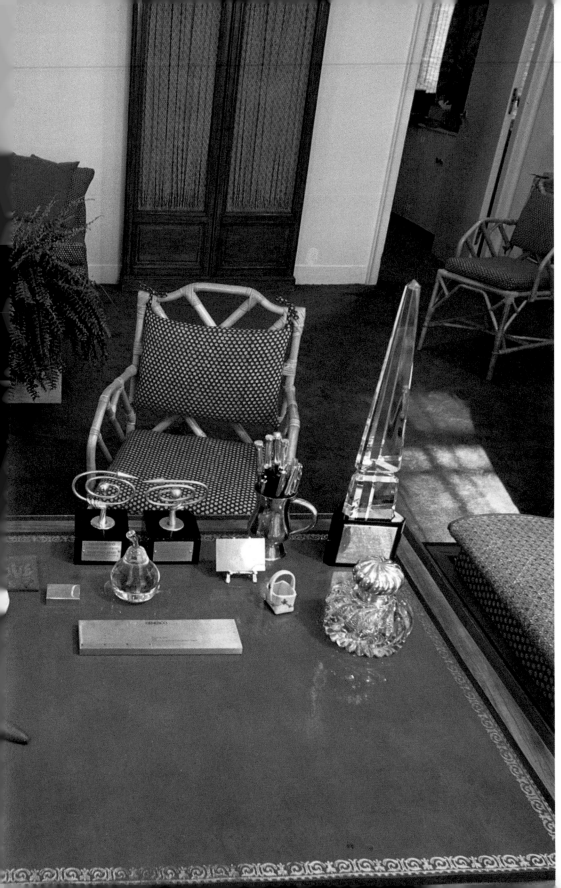

Geraldine Stutz was running Henri Bendel, New York's chicest department store, when women were rare in executive suites; her office reflects her feminine brand of style and strength. The lavish use of contrasting fabrics and bright colors might be distracting in a less creative business—here it's electric. On the wall, an antique armoire opens to reveal a three-way mirror, designed by H. McKim Glazebrook, who also redesigned Bendel's main floor. The informal banquette, piled with pillows, is used weekly for large meetings. The rattan desk chair and the visitors' chairs are identical, suggesting equality. Rattan, normally too casual for executive use, works here. Ms. Stutz solves the problem of storage by using the round storage basket at her feet.

Here is your basic-black-and-chrome, get-down-to-business office—but with a big difference. Most executives like to make it clear who's in charge behind the desk and who's just visiting: Lee Berendt, president of Commodity Exchange, has chosen an oval table instead of a desk. Only the desk chair from Atelier International and the guest chairs from Krueger indicate that there are degrees of power here.

One-time Southerner Larry Nachman moved the New York offices of Swirl, a company that manufactures loungewear designed by Bill Tice and others, to Rockefeller Center because he wanted to be able to open his windows. With cross ventilation, aided by something you don't often see in an office—a ceiling fan— he's able to do without air conditioning. The desk chair, English, circa 1840, reupholstered in leather, comes from New Orleans, the town where Mr. Nachman went to college. Along with the plush velvet upholstery of the Knoll guest chairs, and the fan, it makes him feel right back at home.

The Dunbar chair, left, designed by dePolo/Dunbar, and the Karl Springer chair, right, might be pieces of sculpture, yet they remain among the most comfortable available. Both chairs could function beautifully as guest or conference chairs; the Dunbar serves excellently behind a desk as well.

The chair below, of black Claro leather, was designed by
Le Corbusier in 1929 and quickly became a classic. How
effectively it can be used is demonstrated in Edward
Elson's office (pages 28 and 29).

Above, an armchair by Knoll in nickel-finish steel, upholstered in handwoven wool. It won't fit in everywhere, but wherever it's found, it will be a conversation piece. Below, Knoll's Brno chair, designed by Mies van der Rohe. This classic often is imitated, but rarely with much success. The frame here is polished stainless steel.

Two chairs that shine with good design. Above, a Knoll armchair by William Stephens. The gracefulness of the chair's arms, thin laminations of wood veneer, separates it from its many less-expensive imitations. Below, a Knoll swivel-tilt desk chair by Andrew Ivar Morrison and Bruce R. Hannah. The frame and base are of cast aluminum.

The classic Ward Bennett side chair from Brickel. The pull-up chair with its low arms and continuous carved wood frame, upholstered here in leather, is ideal for a conference, guest, or dining chair. It costs about $1100, plus fabric.

Armchair with round carved wood frame of oiled natural ash, knife-edge seat cushion, caned seat and back. Ward Bennett for Brickel, at approximately $1100, plus fabric.

Both chairs above by Ward Bennett. Above left, the Mobius Executive armchair is fully upholstered, with low back and carved wood frame, suitable for use at a desk. Above right, a more casual upholstered armchair for use at conference or dining table. Right is Knoll's small swivel armchair designed by Max Pearson. The base is stainless steel with adjustable swivel and tilt mechanism, upholstery of foam rubber over molded plastic shells. Approximate costs are $1600, $1100, and $800 respectively, plus fabric.

At left, the Barbar Management chair from Atelier International—comfortable, serious, yet still conceived and executed beautifully. At right, an armchair designed by Ben Baldwin of Jack Lenor Larsen, originally for the Ritz Carlton Bar in Boston. The frame is solid maple.

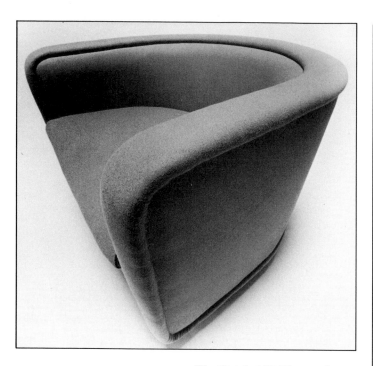

The Brickel U-Chair, shown in two versions, was designed by Ward Bennett in 1977, specifically for the changing, smaller proportions of today's offices. Within small spaces, functional forms usually seem austere and ineffective, taking from an interior rather than adding to it. With a creative sense of design and a rational approach, Bennett designed this chair to fill the gap. The chair is casual and light in scale, and the seamless upholstery gives it a rich look, ideal for reception areas as well as for offices.

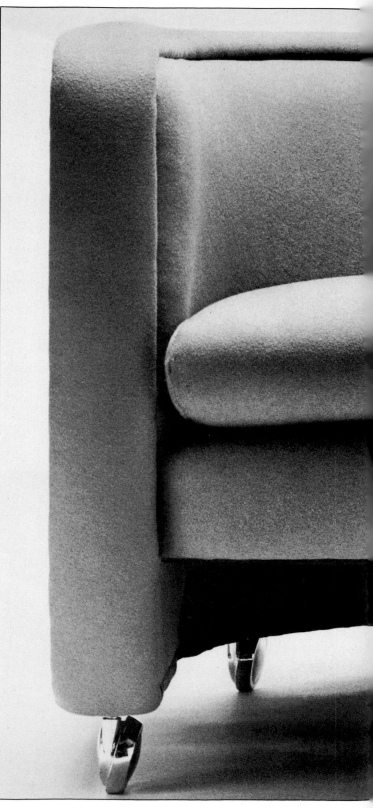

85

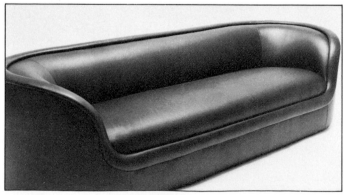

Above, the companion U-Settee, designed by Ward Bennett, is shown here upholstered in a reversible natural-fiber 100-percent Irish tweed, also designed by Mr. Bennett. Each color consists of four to six color fibers. Approximately $1850, plus fabric. Left, Mr. Bennett's Cartouche sofa.

The cartouche was an oval symbol embossed on the possessions of the royal family in ancient Egypt. Whether Mr. Bennett named the sofa to make reference to the shape of the sofa or to the sort of people who can afford to sit in it is hard to say. Approximately $3450, plus fabric.

An extremely rare Queen Anne corner chair, c. 1740, with a highly unusual extra back. This chair, made in Rhode Island, still has the original upholstery on the seat. There are only about six other existing examples of this chair, two in the Henry Francis Dupont Winterthur Museum in Delaware. From Bernard & S. Dean Levy, costing approximately $28,500.

An English George III mahogany exercise chair, or "Chamber Horse," used in the second half of the eighteenth century, from Florian Papp. Originally the seat cushion harbored a set of springs that worked like a bellows, yielding under the weight of a healthy posterior, then pushing back up again as the sitter, with the aid of his arms, sought his rather modest regimen.

TABLES

Unlike desks, tables allow the executive a wide range of expression. Desks almost always are rectangular. Tables can be virtually any shape the imagination can come up with: Consider, for example, Philip Johnson's triangular fantasy for General American Life's conference room (on pages 102 and 103). In dining rooms especially, executives and designers become almost playful. Bob Fomon's office at E. F. Hutton is reasonably sober; yet in the Hutton dining room (pages 114 and 115) the table is of pink granite. There are a number of reasons for this freedom: Conference rooms and dining rooms are group rooms that don't require "power positions." And the table in a conference room or dining room almost always is the only major shape—it doesn't have to go with anything or play second fiddle. Not so in the office itself, where it's important to make sure the table complements the desk and doesn't fight with it. But even there a wide range of shapes is possible, and one superb small table can be an island of style in an otherwise standardized office.

The office of Katharine Graham, chairman of The Washington Post Company, was designed to her specifications; an informal seating area was a high priority. Above, that area, as photographed from her desk; the sofa and lounge chairs are by Knoll, the guest chairs by ICF, upholstered in taupe suede. At right, the adjoining private dining room–conference room carries out the brisk, cheerful feeling. Like Mrs. Graham's office, it is a relaxed and friendly but businesslike room. The table, custom made by Lehigh-Leopold, has an opaque lacquer top; the chairs are by Knoll, upholstered in wool. An executive dining room need not be, and often is not, forbidding or imposing. Guests can, and should, make the room.

Anspach Grossman Portugal is in the design business, creating corporate identities, including logos —Citibank's is theirs, and so are AMF and Continental Group Ltd. Not surprisingly, Gene Grossman's office is clearly elegant, a perfect blending of a few fine elements. The Apollo leather-topped table serves as desk and conference table; Mr. Grossman also uses his drawing board as a desk. The executive chair is the Knoll classic Pollock chair; the three guest chairs are by Mies van der Rohe. The single ficus tree adds warmth and color to the room.

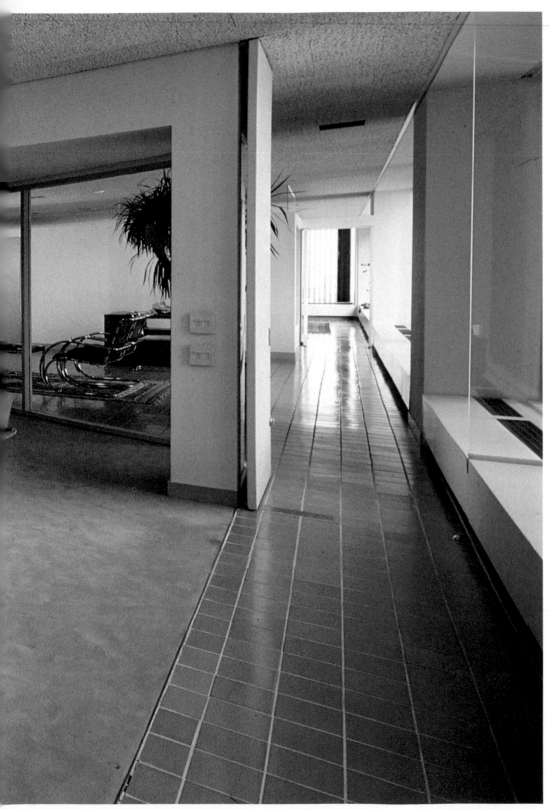

Interconnect Planning Corporation manufactures telephone systems of the future. Its conference area keys into that image with minimal elements, all of them functioning optimally. The chairs are burgundy-covered Knoll Brno chairs. The table of Russo Verde marble seems to grow from the cut-velvet carpet. Though expensive, marble conveys the feeling of luxury and permanence as few materials do; it is especially effective in a conference room.

The triangular building that headquarters General American Life Insurance Company, the largest life insurance company in Missouri, was designed by Philip Johnson (the Museum of Modern Art in New York and the Pennzoil Building in Houston are among his other achievements). Mr. Johnson also oversaw the interior furnishing of the offices. The echoing triangular table in the conference room is of three-inch-thick granite from Italy, its base of brass. The walls are covered in brown Ultrasuede.

The boardroom of the Banco di Roma is a study in luxury—an Italian red Lavanto marble table that rests on a steel base, leather chairs by Zographos. The custom-loomed carpet carries out the design of the diamond-shaped columns on the exterior of the building.

Another conference room, another bank, another table—but again an aura of permanence and substance: The boardroom of the First Atlanta Corporation gives one the sense that the institution and its members have been here for a long time and will be here for a long time to come. When the bank holding company, founded in 1865, moved in 1969 from its original building, the boardroom was painstakingly reconstructed, piece by piece; the bank built an exact replica. The wood paneling is pecan, bleached to the color in the original boardroom. The Oriental rug removes the institutional feeling of any office and creates a beauty of its own.

Three of the dining rooms at the J. Henry Schroder Bank in New York are referred to by Chairman Mark Maged as the Green Room, the Gray Room, and the Red Room. The differing color schemes, table shapes, furnishings, and art create three strikingly different environments. The Gray Room, near right, centers on a dining table made of burl wood. On the walls are prints by Dieter Roth and Joseph Albers.

The table in the Green Room, above, is of Verde Acceglio marble, custom-designed by Ferguson Sorrentino. Chagall lithographs animate the room. The Red Room's tulip table and chairs were designed by Eero Saarinen. The art in the dining rooms, as throughout the bank, was chosen carefully, not ordered indiscriminately to match the decor, an unfortunate tendency of many corporations. The china used in all the dining rooms is made by Royal Worcester and incorporates the Schroder family crest.

Again, an office doesn't have to be large to be well designed. Golo Footwear Corporation, like many manufacturing companies, must devote most of its space to its showroom selling area, and so individual offices tend to be small. In the office of president Arthur Samuels, Jr., the horseshoe-shaped desk was custom designed to serve two functions, as conference table and desk. The desk is of practical, easy-care Formica laminate. Surrounding the desk are the famous Pollock chairs from Knoll.

Some boardroom tables have invisible built-in speakers. In this board-room the speakers seem to add to the power of the place.

One would hate to come unprepared to a meeting in so awesome a room, the boardroom of Crocker National Bank in Los Angeles. Much of the room's effect comes from the richness of the materials. The U-shaped table, which seats 28, was designed by Bert England, and is of highly polished bartiki wood. The stripe of light on the rug leads like a red carpet to the seat of power in the room. In the reception area, above, the custom-designed reception desk incorporates a well-integrated communications and security system.

The conference table at left, designed for Sunar by Douglas Ball, has a top of imported Verde Antique marble, one and one-half inches thick, with a bull-nose edge. The base is steel in a matte-black finish.

The Thonet table above has a tubular chrome base with self-leveling glides and a self-edged plastic laminate top. Its modest price—$240 —makes it an excellent example of first-rate design at a reasonable cost.

The Kyoto coffee table from Sunar is made of beech-wood with rosewood inlay. The criss-cross pattern is reminiscent of a Japanese temple. The price is approximately $5000.

Castelli's LC table, shown here with dark walnut top and tubular chrome base, was designed to be "the focal point of a room." Castelli's parent company, Anonima Castelli, was started in Italy in the latter part of the nineteenth century as an artisan workshop. Castelli Furniture came to the United States in 1974. Italy's emergence during the last decade as the dominant force in consumer products design has already been seen in the work of every other European country and now is having its effect in the United States.

The conference table, forty-eight inches in diameter and suitable also as a table-desk, has a graceful, mirror-polished stainless steel base. The bullnose-edged top of this table from Zographos is of marble, available in several shades.

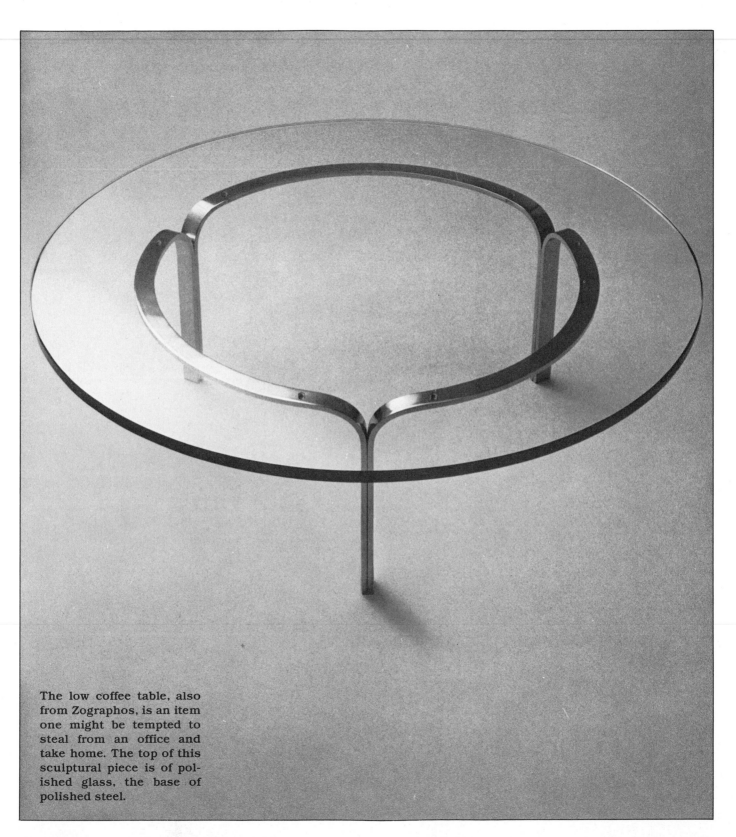

The low coffee table, also from Zographos, is an item one might be tempted to steal from an office and take home. The top of this sculptural piece is of polished glass, the base of polished steel.

The La Basilica table from Atelier International is an up-to-date refectory table, designed by Mario Bellini, and made in a special natural Italian walnut with a variety of light-to-dark sapwood colorations. The cost is approximately $3800.

LIGHTING

It used to be, all you asked of the lights in your office was that they turn on. No longer! As today's executives realize, lighting shapes the look of an office more than a view, more even than furniture. The most expensive decor can lose all subtlety and depth under glaring illumination; the simplest office may acquire an elegance in soft chiaroscuro. For most offices, the less lighting the better, but choices are still as varied as, well, the spectrum.

Notice, for instance, the natural light of J. Howard Johnson's office (pages 140–141), the play of artificial light in the offices of the Williams Companies (pages 154–155), the neon sculpture in the screening room of George Barrie of Fabergé (page 137). Most senior executives prefer not to clutter their desks with lamps, and so most lighting is indirect—recessed incandescent ceiling lights provide the most unobtrusive illumination. However, hanging° lights, when they're attractive, can be an important design element, and exposed track lighting, especially in a modern office, can add to the room's appeal. The only kind of lighting to avoid is fluorescent. No matter how muted or recessed it is, fluorescent light shrieks of mass production, is dreadful to work by, and makes both the room and the people in it look ghastly. If you have fluorescent lights, turn them off and use lamps instead. Natural lighting is a big bonus—it's the nicest and most restful light. For that reason, window treatments should be kept simple: neutral vertical blinds, slim horizontal blinds, or light curtains make the most of natural light. If the windows open onto a view, don't feel compelled to cover it up.

Fabergé is a cosmetics company with brands "Babe" and "Brut" and its eye on the future. The office of Chairman George Barrie uses dramatic spotlighting to throw into relief the exciting architectural lines and modular furniture that emphasize the company's theme.

Above, the bathroom, which carries out the space-age design of Mr. Barrie's office suite. The door closes with the push of a button. At right, a neon sculpture is found in the screening room where commercials are previewed.

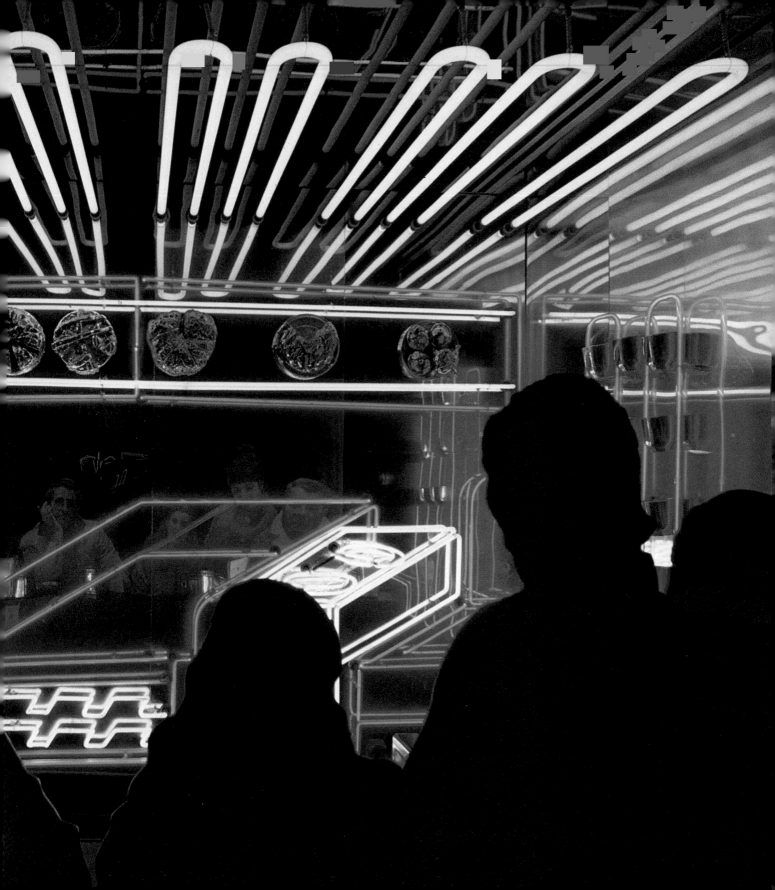

When the Bank of Tokyo acquired the Southern California First National Bank of San Diego to become California First Bank, the international and commercial strengths of the Japanese institution melded with the retail banking acumen of the American. In the office of Masao Tsuyama, chairman of the board of the California First Bank, East meets West once more. The use of venetian blinds as a divider between Mr. Tsuyama's office and those of the bank's senior officers creates a play of light within and without that transforms the room itself into a sculpture of sunshine and shadow.

Above, a granite-top table by Cedric Hartman reflects some of the sparkle.

Washed by sunlight, the office of J. Howard Johnson, president of the Unitrex Division of Merchants Corporation of America, combines ornate architectural detail with the best of modern design. The blues, beiges, and tomato reds animate the paneled walls and plasterwork ceiling in this Fifth Avenue penthouse office. The ceiling, invisible in most offices, here is almost a centerpiece. Notice how meticulously the recessed lighting has been integrated into the plasterwork design.

A carefully achieved marriage of natural and artificial lighting makes the dining room of IBM's Management Development Center a pleasant place in which to lunch. The natural wood of the chairs and the stone walls contribute to creating a country ambience beneath sleek contemporary chandeliers.

Founded in 1896, Sperry and Hutchinson is the parent company to one of the largest furnishings manufacturing groups in the country. The intimacy of the meeting area in the office of Chairman James T. Mills is enhanced by the softly diffused light cast by two handsome porcelain lamps. The hue of the petaled lamp bases picks up the color of the coffee table, constructed of wood covered with linen and lacquered. The walls, sofa, and two love seats are covered in a slubbed wool; the Oriental rug repeats the colors of the handwoven wall hanging, creating the illusion that the two are one continuous, harmonious element. It is the lighting, varied rather than constant, that animates and accentuates the warm textures in this room.

Designed by Tom John (better known for Broadway, movie, and television sets, which include *The Wiz*, *Sybil*, *Taxi*, and *Good Morning, America*), the dramatically lighted entrance hall to the office of Warner Bros. chairman Ted Ashley prepares the visitor for the glamour within. The silver-plated doors once graced a downtown Los Angeles art deco skyscraper. The copper borders were added to extend the doors' size. Above, in Mr. Ashley's office, sunlight streams in through windows rescued from the set of a film entitled *Hotel* and installed here in place of a blank wall. Mr. Ashley's desk, made in Paris, is of stainless steel with a glass base, reversing the usual pattern.

Illuminating an impressive collection of art deco furnishings and *objets* in Ted Ashley's office is a dazzling three-tiered lighting fixture. The art deco brass cabinet on the wall, right, is from the Newell Galleries; the mirror on the wall, left, was made from two art deco headboards, also from Newell, and the art deco wall fixtures come from South America. The two original art deco chairs are covered in red mohair, making a splash of color in what is otherwise a subdued room, with its gray-flannel-covered walls. Art deco seems almost made to order for the office of a modern-day Hollywood mogul, yet the room, for all its flash, shows taste and restraint.

The entire reception area and stair hall of Wender, Murase & White, a New York City law firm, was designed so that natural light would penetrate through to the offices. Artificial lighting enhances and extends the natural light; the wall-mounted fixtures are an integral part of the American elm paneling. The fixtures are made of concentric spun aluminum rings; a quartz light within washes the ceiling with an even intensity.

The Williams Companies, an energy conglomerate in Tulsa, Oklahoma, has knock-out-your-eye architecture, design, furnishings, and what has to be called "special effects." Left, a detail of the brass balcony railing on the stairway between floors is illuminated by the constantly changing light from the skylight above. The flooring is Verde Acceglio and Saint Florient Rose marbles. Above, the reception garden houses the fountain pool. The sound of gently splashing water and a view of the Tulsa skyline create a tranquil oasis.

Here's an office that's as big as all New York. Ronald Saypol, president of the Lionel Corporation, sits almost literally on top of the world. The muted colors are soothing and form a natural backdrop to the unadorned, unparalleled view. Light glints off the glass-block wall onto the two-tone parchment desk by Karl Springer. The two-level taupe carpeting is from Patterson, Flynn & Martin. The use of plants enhances the suspended-in-the-sky feeling of the room.

156

This conference room, with its glass-block walls, floats like a jeweled island in the center of the Lionel space. The use of glass here to increase clarity and light creates a lofty, airy feeling, but manages not to get in the way of business.

The Barbinis have been glass blowers on Murano, the isle of glassmakers, near Venice, since the seventeenth century. The lamp here and several others shown on the following two pages were done by the Barbini family in collabo-

ration with Lighting Associates. They blend creative Italian design, the most exciting in the field today, with functional American technology. Above, a hanging lamp 22 inches in diameter, saline-etched with a burgundy top and border.

A table lamp by Barbini for Lighting Associates, of hand-blown, saline-etched glass. The shade, which is removable, is of varied thicknesses of white and clear glass; the base is gray-black.

The Taccia table lamp, from Atelier International, has a white-enameled spun-aluminum concave reflector resting on a clear glass bowl. The top tilts easily, making the lamp useful also as a spotlight. Available with a black or natural aluminum base.

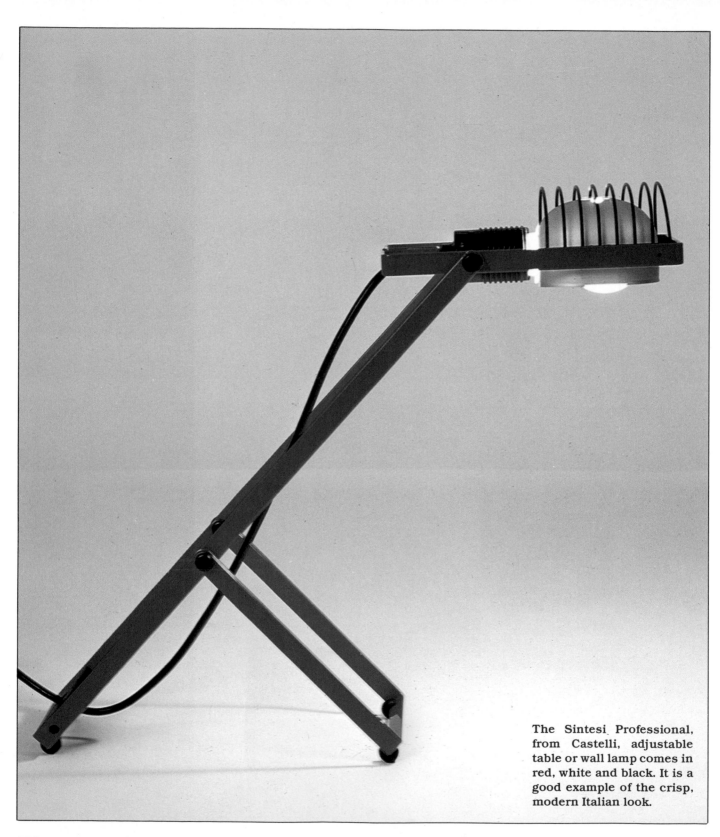

The Sintesi Professional, from Castelli, adjustable table or wall lamp comes in red, white and black. It is a good example of the crisp, modern Italian look.

Made of glass, in colors of amber or rose quartz, this lamp by Barbini looks more like a piece of sculpture as the soft light is suffused through the glass.

ACCESSORIES

Accessories are extras, and to puritan minds, that might make them seem out of place—if not downright distracting—in an executive's office. But accessories can also provide an extra touch of style that transforms an office of mere furniture into a quiet fashion statement. They also announce that whatever role a designer may have played in assembling that furniture, *you* had the taste and panache to make the office your own. Of course, you can also trumpet your lack of taste with pictures of your family (too intimate for an office), awards and diplomas (the best people, we've found in our tour of hundreds of offices, display the fewest), and desk sets and pen and pencil sets (they look pretentious). The major thing to avoid is clutter. Tables and desks ought to be clean and neat and ready for work. Nothing undermines authority more than a mess of last week's memos. Pens and pencils should be in a drawer and not on the desk (unless you have a single, striking pencil holder). Ashtrays should be small and inconspicuous, designed for practicality, not for artistic display. Keep your calculator in a drawer, too; even a telephone ideally should be put out of sight, installed below or on the side of the desk. The few objects on your desk should show your taste, style, and personality—as do the objects in this section, from the sterling silver Georgian skewer used as a letter opener, to the tiny tortoise-shell desk clock. Accessories follow you out of the office as well. Your attaché case, your pen, or your diary can often say as much about you as your clothes.

The offices of Malcolm S. Forbes, publisher of *Forbes* Magazine, might be in a London townhouse, the appointments in a museum. Indeed, this room was designed by architect Thomas Hastings, whose credits include the Frick Museum and the New York Public Library. On the desk are several fine examples of the gold and enamel art of Peter Carl Fabergé, the Russian court jeweler.

The wine cellar, noted for its selection of Premier Cru Lafite Rothschild, marries a sixteenth-century Italian refectory table to twentieth-century Italian Plexiglas chairs. The silver stag-head stirrup cups decorating the beams are from Tiffany and are engraved to commemorate lunches held for leaders of industry and finance. The grilled door, from a Spanish monastery, hides a small pantry. The cellar is occasionally used for corporate luncheons.

The dining room was designed as a setting for two outstanding jewels of Mr. Forbes's collection of *objets:* the nineteenth-century hand-painted Bavarian china and the silver-gilt flatware by Fabergé. The painting is by the late American realist Edward Melcarth.

Halston, the designer, uses the drama of a spectacular view and a spectacular color to create a striking yet elegant office.

The red lacquered table in Halston's office and matching telephone cube were designed by Charles Pfister. In the small photograph, above, a still life of accessories by Halston's friend Elsa Peretti. A silver candlestick, a silver pen on a black nephrite base, and silver objects nestle beside the orchids. Outside the glass walls, the city becomes the ultimate accessory.

You would not know if you were not told that this is the shared conference area of the two senior partners of the law firm Bracewell & Patterson of Houston, Texas. The natural light pouring in through the windows illuminates a superb Dhurrie rug. The telescope emphasizes the unusual and arresting shape of the room, located in the triangular Pennzoil building. Above, the office of partner Searcy Bracewell shows that Early American furniture and accessories can be completely at ease in a modern setting.

Ebony and *Jet* magazines are among the numerous enterprises of John H. Johnson, publisher. A few carefully selected objects highlighted by examples of African art grace this massively proportioned office.

Mr. Johnson's exercise room—complete with barber chair and massage and weight-lifting equipment—an enviable accessory.

The desk of Oppenheimer & Co. chairman Jack Nash is like the bow of a ship. The accessories in this room at the helm of a major brokerage firm are in fact futuristic electronic devices. The office centers on Mr. Nash's command post, from which he can consult, even during meetings, the stock ticker tape recessed in the wall. The leather sofas are from Atelier International, the desk chair from Herman Miller. The floor tile is by Furstenberg.

Remington bronzes and Chinese ivories accent the office of Arthur Rubloff, the real estate developer credited with having created Chicago's Magnificent Mile, on North Michigan Avenue, and also with having designed his own office. The desk, of rosewood and marble, is nine and one-half feet long and five feet wide and so heavy that a steel frame had to be anchored into the rosewood floor to lend sufficient support. Accessories do not have to be priceless to be valuable: To the right of the desk is a brass spittoon purchased for Mr. Rubloff by his father.

In Mr. Rubloff's dining room, the crystal is Waterford, the china Royal Crown Derby, the flatware Pfeiffer Mangasil, the linen place mats and napkins hand-made by Franklin Bayer. The glass-enclosed cabinet houses a paperweight collection, his second. He donated the first, estimated at a value of $4.5 million, to the Chicago Art Institute. Above, choice pieces of crystal rest on top of a hand-carved Oriental table.

An office as full of charm, humor, and hominess as you're likely ever to see—and on top of that, it's part of a cathedral. The Very Reverend James Parks Morton, Dean of the Cathedral of St. John the Divine in New York, uses with commendable panache and effect a late-sixteenth-century Spanish refectory table. The accessories are intensely personal, perhaps the most so, Dean Morton's collection of rocks, gathered in East Hampton and Colorado. This is an office that breaks every rule—and gets away with it.

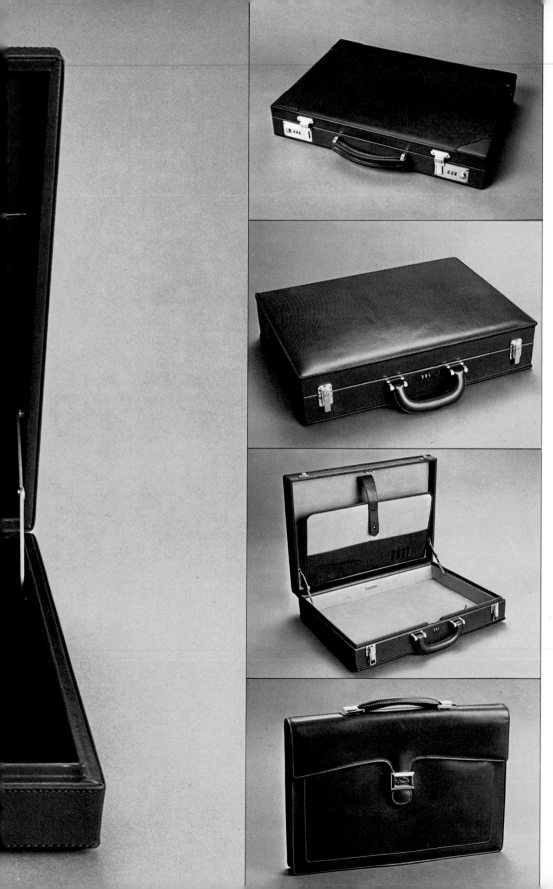

The most important accessory is the attaché case, and the most important color, dark brown or burgundy. Avoid an attaché case emblazoned with initials not your own—they're pretentious and project insecurity. The simplest shape is the best. Avoid a case with disappearing handles—the kind that collapse into the case. Such cases are neither "clutch" nor "professor," and make no clear statement. There are, by the way, no "female" attaché cases; a well-designed attaché case suits both genders equally well. Here and on the next two pages are some of the best examples.

At far left, the very slim English attaché case is made of tan calfskin and available at Alfred Dunhill of London. Approximately $525.

At left, top, a suede-lined briefcase with combination lock. Available at Mädler Park Avenue. Approximately $650.

Second and third from top, shown closed and open, the Bottega Veneta combination-lock pressed-calf attaché case is priced under $375 and has a legal-size file system.

At bottom, a trim, professor-type attaché case in rich teak from Gucci. Approximately $650.

195

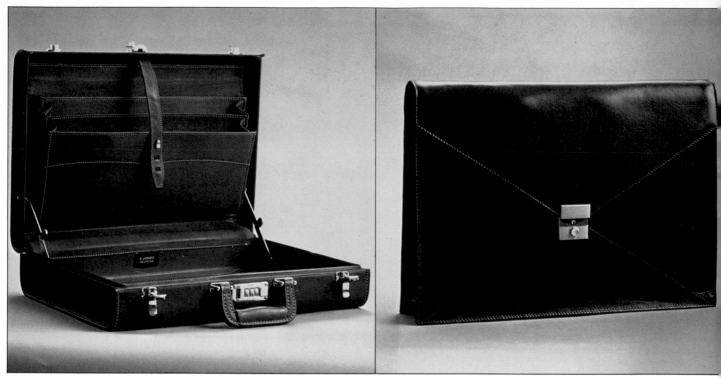

From T. Anthony. Under $450.

This leather folio by Lancel costs under $150.

From Bottega Veneta, a "Limited Edition Folio."
Approximately $550.

A pressed-calf portfolio from Bottega Veneta, shown open
and closed. Approximately $300.

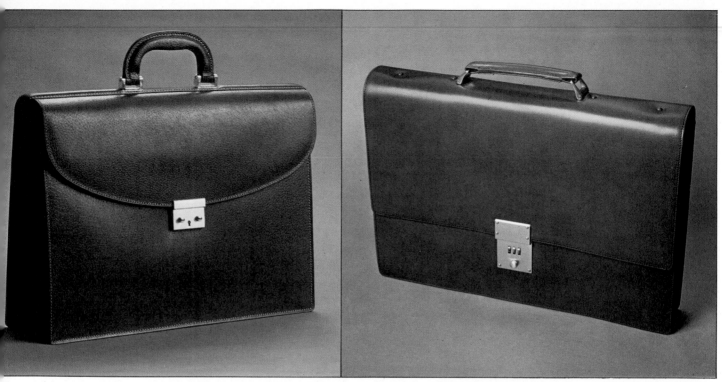

Classic Mark Cross. Under $600.

From Mädler Park Avenue, a "professor" attaché.
Approximately $650.

From Mädler Park Avenue. Under $350.

Hermès' luxurious attaché. Approximately $2000.

Beautiful accessories that can organize your life.

From Mark Cross, a memo pad. Over $100.

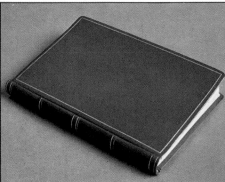

A manuscript book from T. Anthony. Under $100.

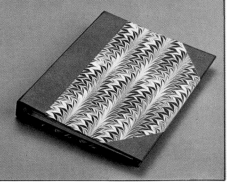

This address book from ffolio 72 can be covered in your favorite paper or fabric. Under $35.

Here the ffolio 72 address book is covered in gray snakeskin. Approximately $50.

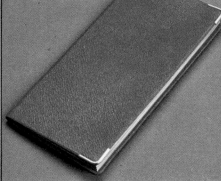

A wallet diary from *The Economist* even includes a section of useful information. Approximately $25.

The Economist desk diary includes international information. Approximately $45.

From Bottega Veneta, an agenda. Under $250.

The Bottega Veneta agenda, open.

S. T. Dupont jotter in tan leather with china-ink black border. Approximately $75.

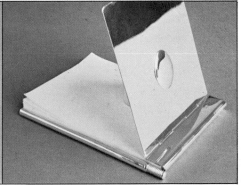

Bottega Veneta's memo and address book. Under $100.

Styled precisely like the manila envelope, only in leather, from T. Anthony. Approximately $50.

Bulgari's sterling silver notepad holder. Under $500.

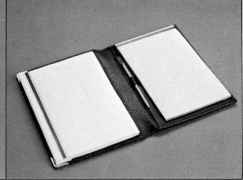

A desk-sized weekly agenda from Bottega Veneta. Under $200.

This notebook of grained calf, from Lancel. Approximately $80.

Gucci's phone desk planner. Approximately $125.

Gucci's pocket diary, covered in pigskin. Under $100.

A brightly colored desk organizer from Leathersmith, Ltd. Approximately $125.

Better than In-Out boxes, these custom-covered folders from ffolio 72. Approximately $25 each.

Timepieces are for information, not decoration. Big clocks are clunky. A clock should be small and inconspicuous, though not so small it can't be read.

Tiffany & Co. Under $200.

Top, Concord electric desk clock. Under $300.
Center, Gübelin gilt and lacquer finish. Under $150.
Bottom, Tiffany & Co. gold alarm clock. Under $200.

Top, Concord 2⅜-inch clock. Approximately $250.
Center, Tortoise-shell clock by Hermès. Approximately $600.
Bottom, Tiffany & Co. gilt with red numbers. Approximately $150.

Top, Gübelin, octagonal eight-day clock. Under $150.
Center, Van Cleef & Arpels chrome and gold plated alarm clock. $650.
Bottom, Cartier burgundy clock. Approximately $250.

Pen and pencil sets are for graduations and retirements. Keep your extra pens and pencils in a drawer or in an attractive pencil cup. If you've got a good-looking fountain pen or an elegant ballpoint, flaunt it. The pens and pencils shown here range in price from the seventy-nine-cent Flair pen—an example of good design when price is no object—to the over-$2000 eighteen-karat-gold "ruler pen" from Bulgari.

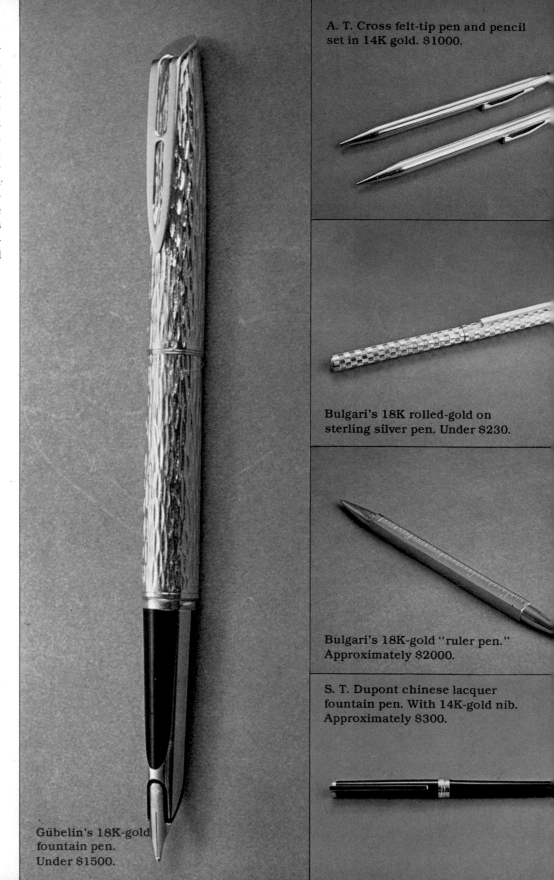

A. T. Cross felt-tip pen and pencil set in 14K gold. $1000.

Bulgari's 18K rolled-gold on sterling silver pen. Under $230.

Bulgari's 18K-gold "ruler pen." Approximately $2000.

S. T. Dupont chinese lacquer fountain pen. With 14K-gold nib. Approximately $300.

Gübelin's 18K-gold fountain pen. Under $1500.

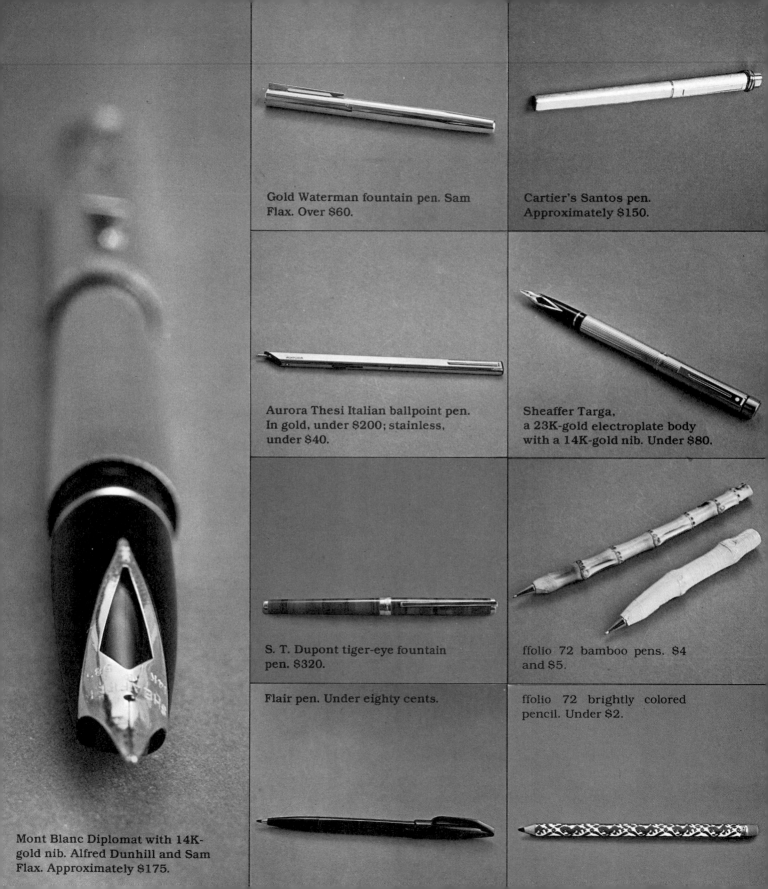

Gold Waterman fountain pen. Sam Flax. Over $60.

Cartier's Santos pen. Approximately $150.

Aurora Thesi Italian ballpoint pen. In gold, under $200; stainless, under $40.

Sheaffer Targa, a 23K-gold electroplate body with a 14K-gold nib. Under $80.

S. T. Dupont tiger-eye fountain pen. $320.

ffolio 72 bamboo pens. $4 and $5.

Flair pen. Under eighty cents.

ffolio 72 brightly colored pencil. Under $2.

Mont Blanc Diplomat with 14K-gold nib. Alfred Dunhill and Sam Flax. Approximately $175.

MIC

STOP
EJECT

SONY

E-IDX

START

As a general rule, the only electronic equipment on a desk should be the telephone. These dictating machines, though, are slim and trim enough to fit into an attaché case or even a flat portfolio.

Left page: Close-up of the Sony BM-12, 15 ounces.

with electronic indexing. The pocket-sized recorder can record continuously for up to eight hours and also can record directly from a radio or television. Under $370.

Above left is the side view of the Sony BM-12.

At right is the smallest

Sony ever—the Sony BM-500, weighing in at 9 ounces. The rugged little recorder is protected by an attractive black all-metal case, making it perfect for dictating while you're jogging or playing tennis. Under $300.

Above left is the pocket-size Micromite from Dictaphone, featuring a "Q-Alert" system that lets your secretary know, when transcribing, how long each letter is. Under $300.

Above right, you can't get any lighter than this. Norelco's 640 Impromptu pocket recorder weighs 6.5 ounces. Approximately $325.

On the facing page, top, the Norelco UltraSlim Executive Notetaker weighs 8.2 ounces and is only three-quarters of an inch thick. Optional accessories include a telephone adaptor and a conference micro-

phone. Approximately $275.
Bottom, IBM's Executive
Recorder is competitively
priced under $200.

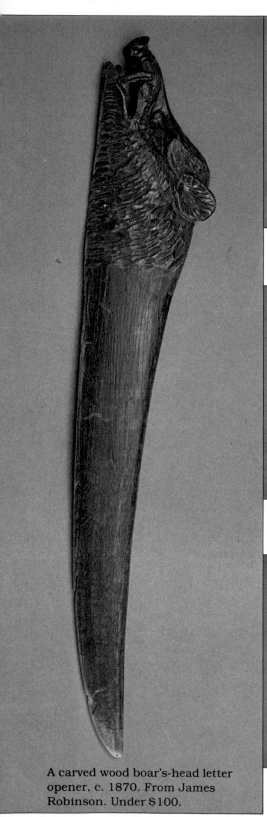

A carved wood boar's-head letter opener, c. 1870. From James Robinson. Under $100.

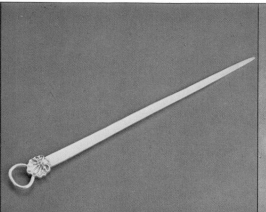

A George III silver shell skewer, now a letter opener. James Robinson. Under $750.

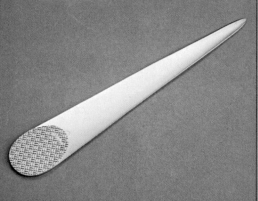

Gübelin's 18K yellow gold and stainless steel letter opener. Approximately $450.

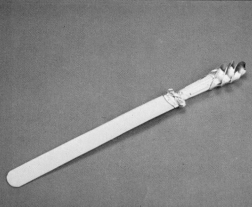

A Victorian silver-mounted ivory paper knife, c. 1889. James Robinson. Approximately $375.

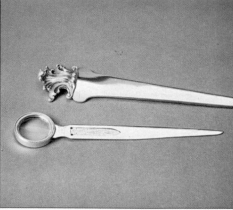

Buccellati: A handmade silver letter opener; a magnifying glass/bookmark/letter opener. Price unavailable.

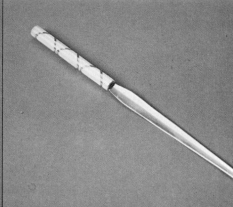

Cartier's sterling silver letter opener with fluted handle and 18K-gold ribbon work. Approximately $300.

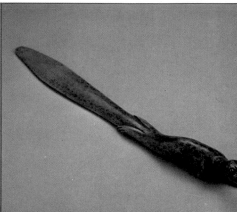

A Victorian carved and painted wood seal from James II Galleries at James Robinson. Under $150.

The perfect desk ornaments are as functional as they are decorative.

Featured on this page are Victorian magnifying glasses, all from the James II Galleries at James Robinson, approximately $300 each. At top, a shagreen and ivory handle. Middle, tortoise and porcelain handle. And bottom, carved wooden handle.

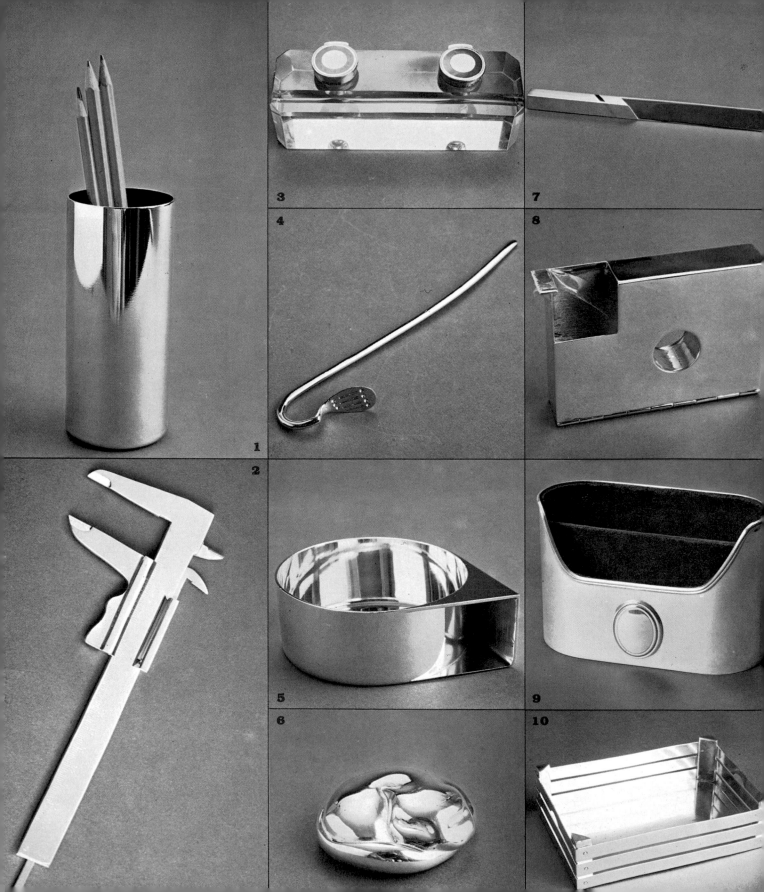

On both pages, a potpourri of beautiful yet functional desk accessories.

1 Polished-chrome pencil holder—TSAO Designs.

2 Sterling silver architectural ruler—Mark Cross.

3 An Edwardian silver and enamel mounted glass inkwell—James II Galleries.

4 Gold-plated bookmark—Mark Cross.

5 A sterling silver bowl which can be used as an ashtray or paper clip holder—Bulgari.

6 Sterling silver sleeping cat paperweight—Tiffany.

7 Sterling silver and 18K gold inlaid letter opener—Bulgari.

8 Sterling silver Scotch tape holder—Tiffany.

9 Sterling silver letter holder lined in midnight-blue velvet—Cartier.

10 Small silver openwork basket to hold business cards—Tiffany.

At right, three ashtrays from TSAO Designs.

11 Polished greenstone marble.

12 Polished chrome.

13 Polished black marble.

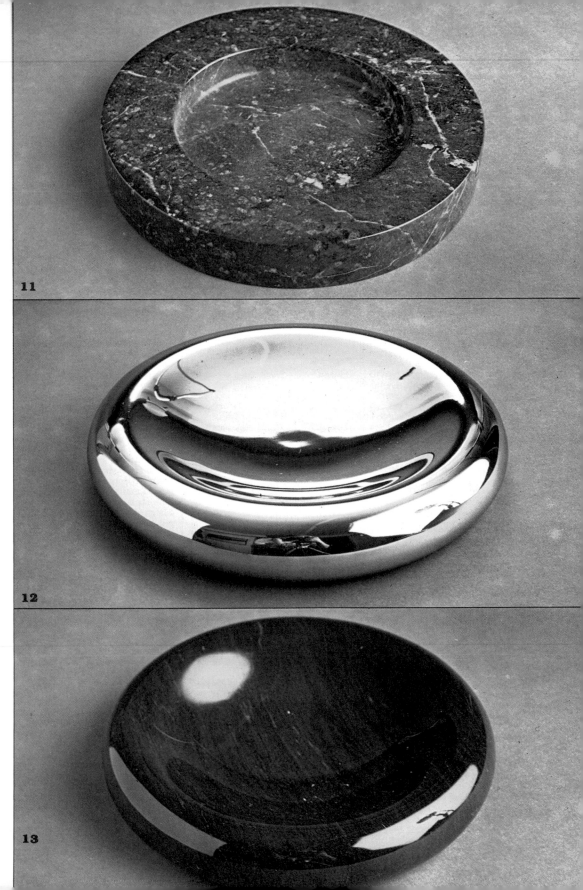

11

12

13

business information
Price: Approximately $45

Bottom left and middle
Bottega Veneta
Agenda, address book, memo pad,
and calculator
8″ x 9″ x 1½″
In pressed-calf desk or traveling
case, refills available
Item #3143
Price: Under $250
Shown with sterling silver
magnifying glass with ribbed
handle, 2 gold plate bands, for
$155 (Item #6096); sterling silver
felt-tip pen, lizard pattern, with
clip, at $100 (Item #6063); and
sterling silver ballpoint pen, rope
design with gold-plated trim, for
$165 (Item #6067), sold separately

Bottom right
S. T. Dupont
Jotter
China-ink black border
Saks Fifth Avenue, Lord & Taylor,
Bloomingdale's
Item #50011
Price: Approximately $75

Page 199

Top left
Bottega Veneta
Memorandum and address book
Item #3148
6½″ x 8¾″
Pressed calf, snap closing, refills
available
Price: Under $100

Top center
T. Anthony Ltd.
Manila-style envelope
Letter size, in burgundy, dark
brown or tan leather
10″ x 13″
Price: Approximately $50

Top right
Bulgari
Notepad holder with pen
Item #621044
Sterling silver
Price: Under $500

Middle row, left
Bottega Veneta
Weekly agenda and address book
Item #3100
9″ x 11½″
Large size, pressed calf, refills
available
Price: Under $200

Middle row, center
Lancel
Legal-size notepad case
Item #10-30-81
Price: Approximately $80

Middle row, right
Gucci Shops
Phone desk diary

Item #021-116-1330
Combination address book and
appointment calendar; pigskin,
neat metal corners
Price: Approximately $125

Bottom left
Gucci Shops
Executive planner
Item #034-143-58
Address book, diary, and notepad
in pigskin breast-pocket wallet
Price: Under $100

Bottom center
Leathersmith TM of London, Ltd.
Desk organizer and document case
Item #DO1/3H
Envelope style
Price: Approximately $125

Bottom right
ffolio 72
Linen portfolios for desk
Beige with brown, green with green
Price: Approximately $25 each

Page 200

Tiffany & Co.
Alarm clock
Item #4062/54-124
1½″ diameter
Gilded brass finish, quartz
movement
Price: Under $200

Page 201

Top left
Concord Watch Corporation
Desk clock
Item #87-533-76
H: 5¼″ W: 4⅞″ D: 2⅜″
Electric; day date; brushed yellow
brass, polished front plate, silvered
dial
Price: Under $300

Left column, center
Gübelin
Alarm clock
3″ x 3″
Jaccard square burgundy lacquer,
8-day movement, gilt and lacquer
finish
Price: Under $150

Bottom left
Tiffany & Co.
Desk clock
Item #9062/53-247
Quartz, gilt finish with brushed
silver dial, alarm
Price: Under $200

Middle column, top
Concord Watch Corporation
Ring clock
Item #82-182-76
2⅜″ diameter
Polished yellow brass, 8-day
movement with alarm
Price: Under $250

Middle column, center
Hermès
Infante
Item #1074
3″ x 3″
Oval, set in tortoise shell
Price: Approximately $600

Middle column, bottom
Tiffany & Co.
Square alarm clock
Item #9059-1-200
3″ x 3″
Gilt with red numbers, 8 day, 15
jewel, alarm
Price: Approximately $150

Top right
Gübelin
Octagonal clock
3″ x 3″
Gray lacquer, 8-day movement, gilt
and lacquer finish
Price: Under $150

Right column, center
Van Cleef & Arpels Inc.
Palm Beach, Beverly Hills
Alarm clock
Item #33V171-4
3″ diameter
Chrome and gold plated, brushed
silver dial
Price: Approximately $650

Bottom right
Cartier, Inc.
Palm Beach, Houston, Beverly Hills
Square travel clock
Item #57-61232
3″ x 3″
Burgundy enamel, brass overlay, 8
day, wind alarm
Price: Approximately $250

Page 202

Right
Tiffany & Co.
Patek Philippe Naviquartz marine
chronometer in case
Item #9063/2-25
5″ x 6½″
Mahogany with brass corners and
two incut brass plates
Price: Approximately $3500

Left
Case for clock

Page 203

Left
Tiffany & Co.
Baume & Mercier carriage clock
Item #9069/4-103
3½″ x 1½″
Octagonal chronometer in
pearwood case with brass fittings,
octagonal inscription plate inside
top, pigskin carrying case
Price: Approximately $3000

Right
Case for clock

Page 204

Left
Gübelin
Fountain pen
18 karat yellow gold, handmade
bark finish
Price: Under $1500

Top right
A. T. Cross Company
Pen and pencil
Item #8001
Solid 14 karat gold
Price: $1000

Right, second from top
Bulgari
Felt-tip pen
Item #760657/1
18 karat rolled gold on sterling
silver
Price: Approximately $230

Right, third from top
Bulgari
Ruler pen
Item #760702
18 karat gold, extendable to 36
inches, 2 ink colors
Price: Approximately $2000

Bottom right
S. T. Dupont
Fountain pen
18 karat gold nib; black Chinese
lacquer case
Item #46274
Price: Approximately $300

Middle
Mont Blanc Diplomat
In New York available through
Alfred Dunhill of London, Inc.
and Sam Flax
Classic fountain pen; black with 14
karat gold trim and clip, lifetime
guarantee
Price: Approximately $175

Page 205

Top left
Waterman fountain pen
In New York available at Sam Flax
23.3 karat gold electroplate pen, 18
karat gold nib
Price: Over $60

Left, second from top
Aurora Thesi ballpoint
In New York available at Sam Flax
Flat, very thin gold, made in Italy
Price: Gold, under $200; stainless
steel, under $40

Left, third from top
S. T. Dupont
Fountain pen
Tiger eye, 18 karat gold nib
Item #46281
Price: Approximately $320

Bottom left
Flair

Felt-tip pen
Price: Under 80¢

Top right
Cartier, Inc.
The Santos pen
Ballpoint in stainless steel
Price: Approximately $150

Right, second from top
Sheaffer Targa
In New York available at Sam Flax
Fountain pen; geometric pattern,
14 karat gold nib, body 23 karat
gold electroplate
Price: Under $80

Right, third from top
ffolio 72
Bamboo pens
Large and small
Price: $4 and $5

Bottom right
ffolio 72
Pencil, covered with paper
Price: Under $2

Page 206

Sony
BM-12
Portable dictator
15 oz.
Standard pocket size
Price: Under $370

Page 207

Left
Sony BM-12, close-up (see above)

Right
Sony
BM-500
Microcassette, pocket-size
notetaker
9 oz.
Price: Under $300

Page 208

Left
Dictaphone
Micromite
6½" x 3½"
Uses tiny microcassettes, 60
minutes of dictation on each
cassette; "Q-Alert"
Price: Under $300

Right
Norelco
640 Impromptu
6.5 oz.
5⅛" x 2⅛" x ¾"
The world's smallest, lightest
pocket recorder
Price: Approximately $325

Page 209

Top
Norelco
NT-1 UltraSlim Executive Notetaker
8.2 oz.
5¼" x 2 ⁷⁄₁₆" x ¾"
Price: Approximately $275

Bottom
IBM
Executive recorder
Price: Under $200

Page 210

Far left
James II Galleries at James
Robinson, Inc.
Letter opener
Item #M3115
Carved wood boar's head;
Victorian, c. 1870
Price: Under $100

Top left
James Robinson, Inc.
Letter opener
Item #3372C725 L1755
Silver shell skewer, George III,
London, 1775
Price: Under $750

Left column, center
Gübelin
Letter opener
18 karat gold and stainless steel, 8
inches
Price: Approximately $450

Bottom left
James II Galleries at James
Robinson, Inc.
Paper knife
Victorian, Birmingham, 1889;
silver mounted ivory paper knife
Price: Approximately $375

Top right
Buccellati
bottom: magnifying glass,
bookmark and letter opener;
handmade, 7¾" long
Item #2918
top: letter opener; handmade
sterling silver heavily engraved,
sculptured, baroque style
8½" long
Item #2181

Right column, center
Cartier, Inc.
Letter opener
Item #620097
Sterling silver with 18 karat gold
ribbon work
Price: Approximately $300

Bottom right
James II Galleries at James

Robinson, Inc.
Letter opener
Item: #M3144
Victorian, carved and painted
wood, c. 1875
Price: Under $150

Page 211

Top
James II Galleries at James
Robinson, Inc.
Magnifying glass
Item #M3091
Victorian, c. 1890; shagreen and
ivory handle
Price: Approximately $300

Middle
James II Galleries at James
Robinson, Inc.
Magnifying glass
Item #M3048
Victorian, c. 1885; tortoise and
porcelain handle
Price: Approximately $300

Bottom
James II Galleries at James
Robinson, Inc.
Magnifying glass
Item #M3092/6
Victorian, c. 1870; carved wood
handle
Price: Approximately $300

Page 212

Top left
TSAO Designs Inc.
Pencil holder
Item #PH-1
2" diameter x 4" high
Polished chrome
Price: Approximately $35

Bottom left
Mark Cross
Architectural ruler
Sterling silver
Price: Approximately $700

Middle column, top
James II Galleries at James
Robinson, Inc.
Inkwell
Edwardian silver and enamel;
Birmingham, 1907
Price: Over $400

Middle column, second from top
Mark Cross
Bookmark
Item #CP4675
Gold-plated
Price: Under $30

Middle column, third from top
Bulgari
Bowl/ashtray
Item #620053/9

Modern sterling silver
Price: Approximately $150

Middle column, bottom
Tiffany & Co.
Paperweight
Item #2703/25559
2" diameter
Sterling silver sleeping cat
Price: Over $500

Top right
Bulgari
Letter opener
Item #621051/1
Sterling silver and 18 karat gold
inlaid geometric design
Price: Approximately $550

Right column, second from top
Tiffany & Co.
Scotch tape holder
Item #206/552
4" x 5"
Sterling silver
Price: Approximately $650

Right column, third from top
Cartier, Inc.
Letter holder
2½" x 4"
Sterling silver, midnight blue velvet
lining
Price: Under $400

Bottom right
Tiffany & Co.
Openwork gallery tray
Item #534/3422
4" x 5"
Sterling silver
Price: Over $325

Page 213

Top
TSAO Designs Inc.
Ashtray
Item #A-7
7" diameter
Polished greenstone marble,
contemporary square-edge profile
Price: Approximately $50

Middle
TSAO Designs Inc.
Ashtray
Item #CA-91
9" diameter
Mirror-polished chrome finish,
rounded profile
Price: Over $60

Bottom
TSAO Designs Inc.
Ashtray
Item #A-6
6" diameter
Polished black marble, rounded
profile
Price: Under $50

Addresses

Alfred Dunhill of London, Inc.
620 Fifth Ave.
New York, NY 10020
(212) 481-6950

Anthony, T., Ltd.
—See T. Anthony Ltd.

A. T. Cross Company
1 Albion Rd.
Lincoln, RI 02865
(401) 333-1200

Atelier International, Ltd.
595 Madison Ave.
New York, NY 10022
(212) 644-0400

Barbini, at Lighting Associates
—See Lighting Associates

Bernard & S. Dean Levy Inc.
981 Madison Ave.
New York, NY 10021
(212) 628-7088

Bottega Veneta, Inc.
635 Madison Ave.
New York, NY 10021
(212) 371-9218
—Also Beverly Hills

Brickel Associates, Inc.
515 Madison Ave.
New York, NY 10022
(212) 688-2233

Buccellati, Inc.
703 Fifth Ave.
New York, NY 10022
(212) 755-4975

Bulgari
2 E. 61st St.
New York, NY 10021
(212) 486-0086

Cartier, Inc.
653 Fifth Ave.
New York, NY 10022
(212) 753-0111
—Also Houston, Bal Harbour,
Beverly Hills

Castelli Furniture, Inc.
950 Third Ave.
New York, NY 10022
(212) 751-2050

Concord Watch Corporation
—See North American Watch
Corporation

Cross, A. T., Company
—See A. T. Cross Company

Cross, Mark, Inc.
—See Mark Cross, Inc.

Didier Aaron, Inc.
32 E. 67th St.
New York, NY 10021
(212) 988-5248

Dunbar Furniture Corporation
601 South Fulton St.
Berne, IN 46711
(219) 589-2111

Dunhill, Alfred, of London, Inc.
—See Alfred Dunhill of London,
Inc.

Dupont, S. T.
—See S. T. Dupont

The *Economist* Newspaper Ltd.
75 Rockefeller Plaza
New York, NY 10019
(212) 541-5730

ffolio 72
888 Madison Ave.
New York, NY 10021
(212) 879-0675

Flax, Sam
—See Sam Flax

Florian Papp Inc.
962 Madison Ave.
New York, NY 10021
(212) BU8-6770

Gübelin, Inc.
745 Fifth Ave.
New York, NY 10151
(212) 755-0054

Gucci Shops, Inc.
685 Fifth Ave.
New York, NY 10022
(212) 826-2600
—Also Beverly Hills,
Palm Beach, Bal Harbour,
Chicago
Toll-free line:
(800) 221-2590

Hermès Boutiques
745 Fifth Ave.
New York, NY 10022
(212) 751-3181
—Also Beverly Hills, Chicago,
Palm Beach, Miami

Hyde Park Antiques, Ltd.
818 Broadway
New York, NY 10003
(212) 477-0033

The Incurable Collector, a
subsidiary of Stair & Company
Inc.
42 E. 57th St.
New York, NY. 10022
(212) 755-0140
—See also Stair & Company Inc.

Jack Lenor Larsen, Inc.
232 E. 59th St.
New York, NY 10022
(212) 674-3993

James Robinson, Inc.
15 E. 57th St.
New York, NY 10022
(212) 752-6166

James II Galleries at James
Robinson, Inc.
—See James Robinson, Inc.

Jordan-Volpe Gallery
457 W. Broadway
New York, NY 10012
(212) 533-3900

Kagan, Vladimir, Designs, Inc.
—See Vladimir Kagan Designs, Inc.

Karl Springer Ltd.
306 E. 61st St.
New York, NY 10021
(212) 752-1695

Kittinger Furniture Company
1893 Elmwood Ave.
Buffalo, NY 14207
(716) 876-1000

Knoll International
655 Madison Ave.
New York, NY 10021
(212) 826-2400

Lancel
690 Madison Ave.
New York, NY 10021
(212) 753-6918

Larsen, Jack Lenor
—See Jack Lenor Larsen

Leathersmith of London, Ltd.
3 E. 48th St.
New York, NY 10017
(212) 752-2690

Levy, Bernard & S. Dean, Inc.
—See Bernard & S. Dean Levy Inc.

Lighting Associates, Inc.
305 E. 63rd St.
New York, NY 10021
(212) 751-0575

Mädler Park Avenue
450 Park Ave.
New York, NY 10022
(212) 688-5045

Mark Cross, Inc.
645 Fifth Ave.
New York, NY 10022
(212) 421-3000
—Also Atlanta, Bal Harbour, FL,
Boston, Costa Mesa, CA, Detroit,
Houston, Palm Beach, San
Francisco, Troy, MI.

North American Watch
Corporation
650 Fifth Ave.
New York, NY 10019
(212) 397-7800

Papp, Florian, Inc.
—See Florian Papp Inc.

Robinson, James, Inc.
—See James Robinson, Inc.

Sam Flax and Co.
551 Madison Ave.
New York, NY 10011
(212) 620-3050

Smith & Watson Inc.
305 E. 63rd St.
New York, NY 10021
(212) 355-5615

Springer, Karl
—See Karl Springer

Stair & Company Inc.
59 E. 57th St.
New York, NY 10022
(212) 355-7620

S. T. Dupont
55 Cambridge Parkway
Cambridge, MA 02142
(617) 492-7676

Sunar
18 Marshall St.
Norwalk, CT 06854
(203) 866-3100

T. Anthony Ltd.
480 Park Ave.
New York, NY 10022
(212) 750-9797

Thonet Industries, Inc.
P.O. Box 1587
York, PA 17405
(717) 845-6666

Tiffany & Co.
Fifth Ave. at 57th St.
New York, NY 10022
(212) 755-8000
—Also San Francisco, Beverly Hills,
Houston, Chicago, Atlanta

TSAO Designs Inc.
31 Grove St.
New Canaan, CT 06840
(203) 966-5528

Van Cleef & Arpels Inc.
744 Fifth Ave.
New York, NY 10019
(212) 644-9500

Vladimir Kagan Designs, Inc.
232 E. 59th St.
New York, NY 10022
(212) 371-1512

Ward Bennett Designs for Brickel
Associates Inc.
—See Brickel Associates Inc.

Wood & Hogan, Inc.
305 E. 63rd St.
New York, NY 10021
(212) 355-1335

Zographos Designs Limited
150 E. 58th St.
New York, NY 10022
(212) 421-6650